# 400+ QUESTIONS TO ASK THE AKASHIC RECORDS

## QUESTION SUGGESTIONS TO FIGURE OUT WHAT YOU WANT TO KNOW AND WHAT YOU WANT TO LET GO

CHERYL MARLENE

SOUL BRIGHT PRESS

**400+ Questions to Ask the Akashic Records**
Question Suggestions to Figure Out
What You Want to Know and
What You Want to Let Go

Published by
Soul Bright Press

Ebook ISBN: 978-0-9825198-9-9

Print ISBN: 978-0-9825198-8-2

# CONNECTING!

I'd love to connect with you!

Please join my newsletter and stay up to date with new books and special offers.

Follow this link:

https://www.cherylmarlene.com/newsletter

# INTRODUCTION

## WHAT ARE THE AKASHIC RECORDS?

You know that eternal part of yourself? Your soul?

Well, as your soul makes its way through the time and space of the universe, its movement creates an energetic record.

This record is your Akashic Record.

When your Akashic Record is opened, you are stepping into the energy of the origin of your soul, turning, and looking at your life from your soul's point of view.

The Akashic Records may be accessed at many levels, across the entirety of all energy flow, potential to form, spiritual to physical. Deep access means that the Reading will be conducted from the soul's point of view and not limited to a physical perspective.

## WHAT IS AN AKASHIC RECORD READING?

An Akashic Record Reading is a telling of the soul's story within the divine knowing of this moment, here, now – and from the soul's perspective.

An Akashic Record Reading always occurs in a unique moment of time. The Reader (the person opening the Akashic Records) is who she is in the moment of opening. The Receiver (the person's Records which are being opened) is who he is in the moment. Neither will be the same person in a day, a month, or a year.

Thus, the Reading presented and received in this moment is only possible in this moment and can never be repeated. This unique aspect fuels the resonance of the Reading and provides foundation for the sacred space of the Reading for both the Reader and the Receiver.

An Akashic Record Reading is always based on the questions and issues the Receiver wants to raise.

Thus, whenever I provide an Akashic Record Reading, before opening the Akashic Records, I invite the Receiver to think of the following:

**What do you want to know?**
**What do you want to let go?**

Within an Akashic Record Reading, this is fundamentally what the Receiver wants from the experience of the Reading.

Either there is something to understand, something which is trying to percolate into awareness, or something both mind and heart are wanting to clarify.

Or there is something which stands in the way of motion forward in life.

Often, there is both: something to know and something to let go.

It is not unusual that the two are related, somehow connected.

## QUESTION SUGGESTIONS FOR ASKING IN THE AKASHIC RECORDS

This book is filled with questions offered as suggestions with the intention of finding the understanding you seek and the ability to release whatever blocks your life path.

Please keep in mind these question suggestions are not "perfect" questions – merely suggestions.

Hopefully these questions will help you focus and define your intention for your Akashic Record Reading.

Plus, these questions are great to use if you are opening the Akashic Records for yourself, or if you are looking for questions to contemplate or meditate on.

## ABOUT QUESTIONS IN A READING

Before your Akashic Record Reading, here's what you need to know about questions:

- There are no wrong/stupid/silly questions.
- If it's arising within you to ask, ASK.
- Avoid self-judgment and self-denial in formulating questions.
- Your question is your question.

Judgment is easy and frequent, thus there is no need to add the stress of asking the "perfect" or the "right" question.

Again, there are no wrong questions.

There is only the question in this moment you want to ask. ASK.

## WHY QUESTIONS?

Simply said, an Akashic Record Reading is based on ASK.

When you ask:

- You establish where your awareness is focused, what concerns you, and where you are ready to listen and accept self-responsibility.
- You are calling forward a specific flow of clarity for yourself.
- You are opening a door, letting go of whatever no longer serves you.
- You are opening to new possibility and accepting a new perspective, releasing the old, outdated, no longer helpful.

Questions demonstrate your willingness to learn.

When life is challenging, control often wants to assert that you know all.

There's that knee-jerk reaction of I KNOW which shuts down all possibility.

When you refuse to consider anything outside the contents of your head, life stagnates.

ASK opens the door to I LEARN.

When you ask a question and you sincerely want to hear a new perspective, you have opened the door to new learning.

Pounding your head on the same brick wall, time and time, again is pointless.

ASK steps you away from the wall and seeks new perspectives.

When you are open to learning, you are in the right place to let go, to listen, to see yourself in a new light, and trust yourself to make a choice about your next step in life.

The questions are organized around the challenges and opportunities of life and begin with the Two Essential Questions and my Twelve Deep Dive Questions.

In Joy!

Cheryl

# TWO ESSENTIAL QUESTIONS

Essentially, all questions boil down to two primary forms. Asking either of these questions is highly effective and will help drill down quickly into any dilemma.

## 1. WHAT DO I WANT/NEED TO KNOW ABOUT XYZ?

This question wants to get to the heart of what isn't seen or understood. XYZ can be anything in life which is troublesome or problematic: you, a challenge in a relationship, the downturn of business, a lack of interest in life, feeling exhausted by the craziness – anything or anyone in life.

This question can take many forms – for example:

- What is my truth about XYZ?
- What is beneficial for me to understand about XYZ?

Framing this type of open-ended question within the concept of truth can help sidestep any inner resistance to clarity. More importantly, this question gets you to the heart of your challenge, brings understanding, and provides clear steps to move your life forward.

## 2. WHAT CAN I LET GO OF XYZ?

Life would be a lot easier if what is true today will be guaranteed to be true five years from now. However, shift and change are the only guarantees. Thus, what worked two years ago may not work today.

This question gets to the heart of this motion by looking directly at what no longer is truthful or in alignment with you. By asking this question, you are giving yourself the opportunity to release the unneeded and move forward.

Other forms of this question include:

- What no longer serves me about XYZ?
- How am I out of step with XYZ?
- What will bring release with XYZ?

# TWELVE DEEP DIVE QUESTIONS

These are process question as opposed to questions digging solely for information. Process means these are questions focused toward the *how* of life. Diving into *how* fuels a process of release. These deep dive questions are the type of questions which can be repeated because they will offer an awesome awareness of personal learning, growth, and integration over time.

---

## 1. WHAT IS MY TRUTH TODAY?

This one question changed my life. For one simple reason: expectations. No matter how many times I ask this question in the Akashic Records, the response is always beyond what I expect or might try to predict. What comes always touches my heart and lifts my spirit, not because the response is easy.

Instead, the response is clear in its depth and encourages me to let go of pesky outdated habits and assumptions based on yesterday's truth. My truth today helps me focus on this moment and identify the next step in my life.

---

## 2. HOW CAN I DEEPEN MY PROCESS OF PHYSICAL-SPIRITUAL INTEGRATION?

The biggest shift is to move from an emphasis on the body and mind to living focused on deep physical-spiritual integration. Integration is not a destination; it is a continual motion of deep learning, growth, and expansion.

---

## 3. IN THIS MOMENT, HOW DO I UNDERSTAND AND CONNECT WITH THE OVERALL MEANING OF MY LIFE?

The most asked question has to do with life purpose and is usually asked within the urge to find the right answer. This push misses so much and can create blinders to the deeper, more supportive perspective of deep soul connection. For most, there is no longer one purpose to life. Instead, there is a dynamic process of living fueled by meaning and clarity in this moment, expanding and integrating to support the choice of next steps.

---

## 4. WHAT CAN I DO TO EXPAND MY ABILITY TO TRUST MYSELF?

In trusting self comes confidence to live life as it comes in the moment. By finding the support to explore deeper edges of trust, life expands beyond expectation.

## 5. WHAT CAN I LEARN TODAY THAT WILL HELP MOVE ME FORWARD IN MY LIFE?

Life is about learning. Learning opens doors and connects life beyond limitation. Every experience is an opportunity to learn. This question can be focused on any life experience or challenge by asking: In this experience, what is there for me to learn?

## 6. HOW CAN I EMBRACE A DEEP SENSE OF SELF-WORTH?

How life experience is understood is directly related to a person's inner sense of worth. Low self-worth drives towards denigration and demeaning interpretation. Swinging too far in the opposite direction, self-worth can push into arrogance and an unwillingness to learn and explore. The deeper road of self-exploration helps you explore the razor's edge between excess and absence.

### 7. HOW CAN I BRING MORE JOY AND LAUGHTER INTO MY LIFE?

Life is also laughter and joy. Take a moment to open your heart and find a new reason to smile.

### 8. HOW DO I HOLD MYSELF BACK FROM FULLY LOVING MYSELF AND OTHERS?

Learn. Laugh. Love. Always. Love is the foundation. When you feel unworthy of love, or feel unable to love yourself, life throws up challenges and opportunities to find ways towards loving expression and experience.

### 9. HOW DOES BLAME SHOW UP IN MY LIFE?

Blame is a pull– really a glue– to the past. Blame wants to keep you focused on the past, stuck there, unable to function in this moment. Blame can be thrown at others, at events, at yourself, at the universe. Blame holds you in check, burdened by a past which needs to be understood and released.

## 10. HOW DOES FEAR IMPACT MY LIFE?

Fear pushes awareness into the future where action in this moment is not possible. What if this happens? What if that happens? What if...? What if...? Frozen in the future, fear blooms around every corner and can paralyze all parts of life. Ask about fear, understand its roots, and then let go. Look fear in the eye and say: There is no room for fear in my life.

## 11. WHAT EXPECTATIONS OR JUDGMENTS DO I HAVE WHICH CREATE BLOCKS OR LIMITS IN MY LIFE?

Expectations are tricky because they can be confused with heartfelt desire. The trouble with expectations is the belief that there is only one way to the desire. Expectation has so strictly defined possible outcomes, the heart is no longer open to possibility, no longer willing to learn. Giving yourself the opportunity to look at expectation in a new way helps you examine closed roads and limitations from a new perspective.

## 12. WHAT ARE MY NEXT STEPS IN LIFE?

Next step – wherever you are in your life, where do you go from here? Let go of limits, believe in yourself, trust you can find and follow your sense of inner truth. How do you take those next steps?

# SOUL POSSIBILITIES

Begin by getting to know yourself from your soul's point of view. I prefer the term soul calling to soul purpose for it has a sense of an energetic flow to connect the shifts over time. The soul's calling in this moment may be different than the awareness of five years ago or in a month or a year.

15. What is my soul's original intention?

16. How can I understand and embrace my soul's calling in this life?

17. What is my soul's calling for me in this moment?

18. In what way can I improve my awareness of connection with my soul?

19. Does my soul carry any bindings which currently hold me back in my life?

20. How can I embrace the soul patterns which serve me in this life?

21. How can I let go of the patterns of my soul which no longer serve me?

22. What am I here to accomplish or create in this life?

23. How can I express my life's passion?

24. What are my gifts in this life?

25. What is blocking my gifts?

# POSITIVE STEPS FORWARD

26. What can I understand, release, or shift to find deeper understanding in my life?

27. What can I do in my life knowing that I won't fail?

28. How do I expand myself?

29. How can I improve my sense of connection with myself, with others, and with the earth?

30. How do I find a sense of spiritual in my everyday life?

31. What are my strengths in this lifetime?

32. What can I do to improve my ability to trust myself?

33. What am I learning about myself as my life changes?

34. What more could I release which would serve my highest expression?

35. What possibilities are opening up for me in my life?

36. Why am I at a crossroads?

37. How can the unexpected expand opportunity for me?

# ADDICTION AND ABUSE – BY ANOTHER

38. What can I understand about my friend's addiction?

39. While maintaining appropriate boundaries, is there anything I can do to support my friend?

---

# ADDICTION OR ABUSE – PERSONAL

40. What is my truth today about this addiction to self-abuse?

41. What do I want when I over consume?

42. What am I not seeing about my situation which would help release my abusive behavior?

43. What am I ignoring through the addiction of self-abuse?

44. To ease or eliminate this addiction to self-abuse, how can I improve my feelings of self-worth?

45. Are there any past or future lives related to this addiction to self-abuse which will help me to understand or release?

# ABUSIVE ACTIONS TOWARDS SELF

46. Why do I feel compelled to hurt myself?

47. How and why do I experience self-hatred?

48. What initiated my abusive action towards myself?

49. What do I gain from hurting myself?

# BURNOUT

50. What one step can I take to ease my experience of burnout?

51. How does a lack of boundaries (either mine or others) contribute to feeling overwhelmed?

52. To relieve burnout, how can I restore emotional and mental resiliency?

53. What helps me feel appreciated in life or in my work?

54. How does disconnection from those I work with contribute to my experience of burnout?

55. How am I unaware of the people around me who appreciate me?

# CAREER, LEADERSHIP & BUSINESS

CAREER

56. Where do I need to focus at work?

57. What can I shift or release so my career moves forward?

58. What am I ignoring that would be helpful to acknowledge about work?

59. What, if anything, can I do to improve sales or profit at my company?

60. Why are my products not selling?

61. What additional education or study would benefit me in my career?

62. What steps can I take to increase my salary or benefits?

63. How would a promotion fulfill me? What steps can I take to be promoted?

64. What do I need to let go of to be more satisfied with work?

65. Why am I restless at work and can't wait for the day to end?

66. What keeps me from being in the present moment at work?

67. How can I convince my boss to allow me to work from home?

68. What do I expect from my boss? What does my boss expect for me?

69. How can I get my boss to be clear about her expectations for my work?

70. How can I improve my relationship with my boss?

71. What does my boss think of me as an employee?

72. How do I deal with the weak management efforts of my boss?

73. To improve our relationships, what do I need to understand about my relationships with my coworkers?

74. Why do I need my boss's approval? From whom else do I need approval?

75. Why am I late to work?

76. What do I not like about my job?

77. What do I fear about my job?

78. Am I safe at work? What will improve my sense of safety or security at work?

79. I'm thinking of finding a new position; what about my current position works for me? What doesn't work?

80. Will I be happier and more satisfied if I change positions?

81. What is most beneficial to look for in a new position?

82. What do I need to release or understand to make a positive job change?

83. How can I improve my dangerous work conditions?

84. Why am I concerned that my position will be terminated?

85. How can I develop the confidence to speak in front of large groups at work?

86. How can I best deal with harassment in my workplace?

87. How can I better handle what feels like a heavy workload?

88. Why do I feel overburdened by responsibility at work?

89. How can I better manage the long hours at work?

90. Why do I feel things are slow at work?

91. What steps can I take to be part of the decision-making process at work?

## LEADERSHIP

92. What are my strengths and challenges as a leader in my business?

93. What holds me back from being an effective leader?

94. What is the truth about the situation within my department in relation to me?

95. What are the dynamics of my team?

96. What are the key aspects of a winning strategy for my team? How can we accomplish our goals?

97. How can I ease tension within my team?

98. What undermines our effectiveness as a team and my effectiveness as a leader?

99. What experiences would encourage greater team cohesiveness?

100. Why do I demand perfection from my team?

101. How can I ease up on myself and others?

---

## BUSINESS OWNER

102. What are the advantages and challenges for me in starting my own business?

103. How is creating my own business in alignment with the meaning of my life?

104. What is the mission of my business?

105. Do I have the capacity to begin my own business?

106. What steps do I take to create a successful start-up strategy?

107. Is now the time for me to begin my business?

108. I am thinking of offering these products or services. How are these in line with the mission of my business?

109. Will the services or products aid in the success of my business?

110. I anticipate challenges – how do I successfully manage and respond to them?

111. What can I shift within myself to move my business into profitability?

112. How is my current business in alignment with my highest expression?

113. What can I do to motivate my employees?

114. What can I do to increase sales in my company?

115. Why is my company losing money?

116. Why are my products or services not selling?

117. What is my exit strategy for my business?

## RETIREMENT

118. Is now the time for me to retire?

119. What do I need to do to prepare for retirement in XX years?

120. What will my retirement look like?

---

# CRIMINAL OR ABUSIVE ACTION TOWARDS OTHERS

121. Why do I feel compelled to hurt others?

122. Why do I dislike myself?

123. How can I connect with my feelings?

124. How can I be more aware of the feelings of others?

125. What initiated my abusive action towards others?

# CRITICAL SELF-IMAGE

126. Is it true that I am not a worthy person?

127. What is the source of my self-criticism or critical self-image? How is this critical self-image held in my mind, body, heart, or soul?

128. Why am I willing to be critical of myself?

129. What can I do to embrace the best of me and release my self-criticism?

130. What can I learn from my self-criticism that will allow me to release its detrimental effects?

131. What about my physical being do I dislike, misunderstand, or am disappointed in?

132. What can I do to shift my critical self-image?

133. What am I carrying that I can let go?

134. What do I get for holding onto this critical self-image?

135. What is the source of strength and power for my critical voice?

---

# DEATH

The release of the physical body to allow the soul to move on is one of the only certainties in life. This event is surrounded by eons of cultural belief, spiritual explanations, and religious dogma. There is resistance and fear. There is judgment and expectation. All rolled up in one event because whatever comes next is not certain.

When dealing with the death of a loved one or the eminent possibility of your own passing, there is no way to avoid your own fears and beliefs. If you are witness to passing, hopefully you'll not want to dump your challenges on the other person nor on other witnesses.

Because at some point, everyone must deal with death either personally or with another, asking the Akashic Records for support is both thoughtful and beneficial.

## SELF-EXPLORATION OF DEATH

Life experience and the early beliefs absorbed from family and society form the fabric of personal thoughts and belief about death until becoming consciously aware and shifting toward a more beneficial perspective.

136. What is my truth about death?

137. What resistance do I have for a death with grace and ease?

138. What is my truth about my own death?

139. What no longer serves me about death?

140. What social or cultural beliefs about death interfere with a peaceful approach to life?

141. What can I do today to make peace with death?

142. How may I explore death on the deepest levels?

143. Am I afraid to die? Why?

144. Am I afraid that someone close to me may die soon?

145. How can I see death as a joyful event?

146. What is beneficial for me to know today about what happens after the physical body releases and no longer functions?

147. What happens to the soul in death?

## TERMINAL ILLNESS – PERSONAL

The exact time of death is usually unknown. However, there are illnesses in which there is no recovery possible. The end is in sight. Thus, the person in this situation is now living with an awareness that is more certain about the time of death. This will make the experience of death a direct part of everyday life. Resistance, futility, anger can be part of the experience as will concern about the effects of death on loved ones. Additionally, the relationship others have with death will affect you and your interactions with them.

148. What expectations, fear, or judgment do I have toward myself about my illness?

149. Do I blame myself for my illness? Do I blame others for my illness?

150. What will help me today to release that which doesn't serve me either in my life or in my passing?

151. What support do I need to pass peacefully?

152. What do I need to acknowledge to myself and to family and friends about my life, my illness, or my passing?

153. How do I make peace with myself in this moment?

154. What is my legacy? How do I pass this legacy on?

155. What resistance do I have to a death with grace and ease?

156. What do I need to do before death?

---

## TERMINAL ILLNESS - ANOTHER

When a friend or family member is confronted with a terminal illness, the limits of what you can do become clear. As a person makes the final choices in their life, the challenges for those who surround them is to be of assistance and support rather than a burden or a hindrance. This can be a very difficult time for everyone and be made worse by the inability to deal directly and honestly with death. We are where we are and, as much of life, the path forward is always in this moment.

157. What can I learn about myself from this person?

158. How has this person been a gift in my life?

159. How do I best support this person in their passing?

160. What words or actions of comfort can I offer?

161. How can I memorialize our connection before this person dies?

162. Is there anything I need to address before this person's passing?

---

## DEATH OF A FAMILY MEMBER

163. Are there any messages for me from this person?

164. Do I hold any guilt about this person's death? How can I release?

165. What is this person's legacy to me?

166. How can I identify and incorporate my grief to help myself move on?

# DISAPPOINTMENT IN SELF

167. Why do I not have a high opinion of myself?

168. Why do I feel that I have failed?

169. What can I do to improve my opinion of myself?

---

## DON'T BELONG ON EARTH

170. Why do I feel like I do not belong on Earth?

171. If I don't belong on Earth, why am I here right now, and where do I belong?

173. What can I do to feel more connected to living on Earth?

# EDUCATION

FOR A CHILD:

173. How can I provide support to my child in the transition into a new school?

174. What type of school will be most beneficial for my child?

175. Why is my child having trouble at school?

---

FOR SELF:

176. What aspects do I look for in a school or educational program?

177. In what way would additional education improve my career prospects?

178. What can I do to be successful in my education?

179. How can I decide on my major?

180. What are the benefits of the school, course of study, or teacher?

---

ISSUES AT SCHOOL:

181. What is at the root of my poor grades?

182. Why is it a challenge to retain information?

183. What is the conflict with my teacher about?

184. Why am I afraid of taking tests?

185. Why do I freeze in completing my schoolwork?

186. Why do I freeze during a test?

---

# FEAR

187. Why am I afraid of XYZ (insert fear)?

188. How is this fear held within my mind, my heart, or my body?

189. What can I do to release this fear?

190. Why does my heart feel trapped or contracted?

191. How does feeling afraid or anxious serve me?

192. What can I learn about fear so that I don't feel paralyzed?

# FEAR OF SUCCESS

Getting exactly what you've dreamed of can be both exciting and terrifying. Excitement unleashed and uncontrolled can lead to egotistical arrogance, while terror can allow the inner critical voice to belittle or denigrate self and take the lead. For most, the fear of success can come from an awareness that there seems to be no balance and that both arrogance and self-judgment may be taking over. Success is a shift in a new energetic expression where balance exists but in a different form than life before. Looking for inner balance is the first step into a new expression of you.

193. What is success for me?

194. Why am I fearful of success?

195. What personal habits or beliefs hold me back from achieving my dreams?

196. In this motion toward success, why do I feel out of balance?

197. Do I have any beliefs about success which no longer serve me?

198. How can I find balance within as I embrace this new motion in my life?

## FEEL EMPTY INSIDE

199. Why does the gap within me feel so big?

200. What steps will assist me in not feeling empty?

201. What is missing in my life or outlook?

202. What do I not understand, ignore, or deny about myself?

203. How are expectations, assumptions, or beliefs related to this empty feeling inside me?

---

# FEELINGS: NUMB OR HARD TO IDENTIFY

204. To what is the lack of feeling or numbness I am aware of in my body related?

205. What stands between me and my feelings?

206. Are my numb feelings related to past trauma?

207. What confuses me about my feelings or lack of feeling?

208. How can I re-store feeling?

209. Am I afraid to feel?

210. What can I shift so that I may begin to be aware of my feelings?

# FINANCES, PROSPERITY & ABUNDANCE

211. Why do I feel financially unstable?

212. What can I release or shift to experience financial stability?

213. What is prosperity for me?

214. Am I missing opportunities of abundance?

215. What can I understand or release about my relationship with money?

216. How can I improve my ability to accept assistance?

217. How is abundance already part of my life?

218. What beliefs do I have which counter prosperity in my life?

219. What is the root of my financial worries?

220. How do I align my life with a clear experience of prosperity?

221. How do I resolve my tax problems?

# HEALTH AND VITALITY

222. What steps can I take to improve my health and extend my lifespan?

223. Is there anything in my environment which is interfering or affecting my health?

224. What type of exercise is most beneficial for me?

225. What type of diet serves my physical and emotional health?

226. How can I create healthy boundaries within my relationships?

# HOLIDAYS

227. What makes a holiday difficult for me?

228. How can I create my own meaningful holiday traditions?

229. What can I view differently about the holidays so that I can enjoy them?

230. What is most important for me to be able to enjoy a holiday?

231. What triggers me during a holiday?

---

# LIFE HAS NO MEANING

232. Why do I feel my life has no meaning?

233. How can I connect on a deeper level with myself?

234. What can I do to reduce the pressure I put on myself?

235. What keeps me from feeling connection with my life?

236. In what way do I feel ashamed about my life?

237. Why do I blame my family or friends for the trouble in my life?

# LIFE STRESS

Defined as the mental and emotion tension and strain resulting from adverse or very demanding circumstances, stress arises in life in response to many situations. The following questions approach stress in a general sense.

238. Why do I feel stress in my heart? (or shoulders, lower back, head, gut, etc.)

239. What is the easiest path toward relieving my stress?

240. For me, how are emotions and beliefs related to stress?

241. What is the primary source of stress in my life now?

242. How does denial contribute to stress in my life?

243. What outdated self-beliefs contribute to stress in my life?

# LONELINESS

244. What is the source of my loneliness?

245. How can I improve my inner sense of awareness so that I don't feel so lonely?

246. How do I reinforce my lonely feelings?

247. How do I find connection with others, with the divine, and with myself?

248. How am I solitary in a positive, supportive manner?

# MOVING TO A NEW HOME

Moving from one home to another maybe the result of circumstances such as a new job, school, or finances, or you may choose to do so because you feel within the need to move.

Whatever your reason, the choice to move either feels right or it doesn't. The move itself is likely to amplify any existing imbalance and may make the move smoother or more difficult. Moving is one of those life situations which can be decidedly negative or absolutely positive.

Wherever you find yourself on this continuum, begin by identifying your personal perspective and any underlying factors which influence the process. This is why the questions focus on the process of the move.

Often the choice to move is the desire to be rid of something. After moving, whatever that was may manifest itself in the new location. Therefore, do your personal work first, and don't expect a move to fix everything.

## SELL, BUY, OR RENT HOME

249. Is now the time to rent, buy, or sell my home?

250. What can I do to make my home transition process proceed with grace and ease?

251. How do I go about finding my new home?

252. What elements am I looking for in a new home?

253. How do I prepare my home for sell?

---

## BEFORE

254. Why do I want to move? Why do I not want to move?

255. If I do not move, what possibilities exist for me in my current home?

256. What holds me where I am?

257. What do I need to release to move literally or metaphorically into a new place?

258. What will help me make a smooth transition?

259. What elements will benefit me in the place to which I am moving?

260. What do I need to shift or release, prior to moving, so that I transition with grace and ease?

261. What are my lessons in this move?

262. Am I in denial about any aspects of this move?

263. What steps can I take to find balance within me through this move?

264. Am I running away from something by moving?

265. Am I clear about the reasons for this move?

266. What steps or plan is most beneficial for a move with grace and ease?

267. How do I involve my family in this move so that they are excited and willing to move?

268. How do I prepare my new home for my arrival?

DURING

269. Is there energy which needs release or to shift in either my current home or my new home?

270. What can I do to make my new home mine?

271. What will facilitate the moving process as I shift from one home to another?

272. Do I have doubts or fears about the moving process?

273. What kind of support do I need as I move?

274. What steps do I take to set up a new home which supports the best of my being and becoming?

---

AFTER (OR IN SETTLING IN)

275. Is there anything to shift or release to feel balance, comfort, and support in my new home?

276. What lessons are available now that I have moved?

277. How do I find alignment and deepest support within the environment of my new home?

---

# PHYSICAL BODY CHALLENGES

278. What am I disappointed in, dislike, or misunderstand about my physical being?

279. What can I do to feel and experience physical vitality?

280. What can I do to shift my critical opinion of my body?

281. What am I carrying that I need to let go?

282. What is the origin of my unease with myself and how is this held in my mind, body, heart, or soul?

283. What benefit do I receive for holding onto a poor self-image?

284. Why do I carry extra weight?

285. How can I release this extra weight?

286. How can I honor and love my body as it is?

# PHYSICAL INCAPACITATION, CHRONIC PAIN OR ILLNESS

287. What is the underlying issue of my physical condition?

288. What do I not know or understand about my physical situation?

289. What resistance do I have to this issue of either physical incapacitation, chronic pain, or illness?

290. Are there any steps I can take or habits I can shift which will help ease or relieve my physical incapacitation, chronic pain, or illness?

291. What is the best way to deal with my guilt, remorse, or anger about my physical incapacitation, chronic pain, or illness?

# PREGNANCY

292. Does my partner want to become a parent?

293. What steps can I take to ensure a healthy and successful pregnancy and a healthy child?

294. Is now a beneficial time to become pregnant?

295. What is blocking my ability to become pregnant?

296. How can my partner best support my pregnancy?

297. How can I best support my partner during pregnancy?

# PROCRASTINATION

298. Why do I put off completing tasks?

299. Is there something for me to understand to be able to move beyond procrastination?

300. Is my procrastination a symptom of a deeper issue?

301. What expectations or assumptions either fuel my procrastination or hinder me from completing tasks?

302. Are my plans for completing tasks realistic or am I expecting too much?

# RELATIONSHIPS

While most of the questions in this section are more focused toward romantic relationships, all of the questions can be directed toward any type of relationship whether that be with a friend, a parent, a child, or a partner.

Every relationship goes through a cycle from beginning to sustaining to parting.

Wherever you are within a relationship, looking to improve or heal relationship is about your awareness of connection and your willingness to explore yourself within the context of the relationship.

Within the Akashic Records the focus is on you: who you are, and what you can do to sustain the relationship in a way which serves both you and your partner.

## FINDING RELATIONSHIP

The number one relationship question in a Reading is: Will I find a partner? If this is the question in your heart, ask.

Know that there are many layers attached to this question which aren't always accessible until one digs deeper. The following questions are the deeper issues which surround the search for partnership.

303. Do I believe I am worthy of the wonderful relationship I desire?

304. What will help the new relationship I desire move towards me with grace and ease?

305. What attributes do I bring to relationship?

306. To be open to a new relationship, what baggage, outdated beliefs, or expectations can I acknowledge and release now?

307. What am I looking for in a relationship?

308. What will help me build greater emotional stability and openness especially within a relationship?

309. How can I learn to be vulnerable?

310. How can I learn to avoid manipulation and coercion in a relationship?

311. What will help me deepen self-trust and trust of another especially within a relationship?

## BEGINNING RELATIONSHIP

The initial stages of a relationship can be fun and exciting, confusing and bewildering. There is the opportunity to find out about the other person as well as yourself. There is also the challenge of working out the relationship without either person giving up self.

312. What will help me connect at a deeper level in my new relationship?

313. What can I learn about myself in this new relationship?

314. Within this relationship, is there anything I am overlooking either in myself or my new partner?

315. What can I offer and receive within this partnership?

316. What can I understand, shift, or release to set this relationship on a path for deep growth and learning?

317. Within this new relationship, what can I do, be, or become to support the fullness of this relationship?

318. What are the potential and possibilities for each of us within this relationship?

## EXPANDING RELATIONSHIP

The expansion stage of a relationship begins when both parties are willing to commit to developing and expanding the relationship. This is not an unconscious stage because the requirement is to consciously step into deepening levels of intimacy and vulnerability.

319. What do I receive in this relationship?

320. What do I provide to this relationship?

321. How can I learn, grow, and expand in this relationship?

322. How does my partner assist me in learning, growing and expanding?

323. What can I understand, release, or support to expand our relationship?

324. Is there anything standing in our way of a deeper relationship?

325. What will bring deeper intimacy to our relationship?

326. What is the dynamic of our relationship?

327. How do we support each other in growth both within the relationship and individually?

328. Within our relationship, how can we improve communication?

329. What am I not seeing about myself or my partner in this relationship?

## STRUGGLE IN RELATIONSHIP

Relationships will have struggles because no two people are the same, and no two people have the same motivations and intentions for their lives. Relationship is always about finding balance. The healthiest approach to take to a struggling relationship is to see the signs of struggle as an opportunity to learn about yourself and about your partner. Taking this approach does not mean that there will be no struggle or that the relationship will continue, but it provides the opportunity to learn and to explore and to expand into who you and your partner are as human beings. The conclusion from this type of exploration may be that the relationship will not be able to sustain itself. At other times, embracing the opportunity of struggle can bring new and deeper understandings which strengthen the relationship and support its continuation.

330. What can I shift or release to move into new understanding about this relationship?

331. Where and how are my partner and I stuck in this relationship?

332. In my relationship struggle, where am I right now with my partner?

333. I feel like I've lost connection with my partner; what is the disconnection about in our relationship?

334. What do I get out of the mean, critical comments that my partner makes toward me? Why does my partner criticize me?

335. To support my relationship, how can I increase my self-confidence and ability to trust myself?

336. What is my truth about the affair my partner is involved in with another?

337. Within the challenges of my current relationship, where and how do I go from here?

338. How do I deal with the pain of my partner's betrayal?

339. How can I understand and release the aspects which bother me in my current relationship?

340. Why am I afraid of my partner? What is my truth in this relationship?

341. How does a lack of communication create struggle for us in this relationship?

342. To move beyond struggle, how can we improve our communication?

343. What is the source of my anger within my relationship?

---

SEPARATION IN RELATIONSHIP

There are moments in relationship when space is needed. In its broadest sense, that is what separation does: offers each person space to contemplate and to explore where they are within the relationship and what their desires are in moving forward. Like any period of struggle, separation may lead to a final parting or to an opportunity to find the deeper path for the relationship to continue.

344. Within our relationship, is there an alternative to separation?

345. In considering a separation, what are the benefits and challenges for us both?

346. How will separation affect our children, family, or friends?

347. How can we soften or alleviate potential damage that a separation may have on us or our family?

348. What agreements would be most beneficial for all involved before, during, and after separation?

349. What are the goals of separation for each of us?

350. How will separation help the struggle of our relationship?

## PARTING FROM RELATIONSHIP

Sometimes the healthiest choice for relationship is to bring it to an end. This can be difficult and painful for both parties and for family and friends who are connected through the relationship. When possible, dealing with the blame, fear, judgment, or anger there might be within yourself or towards your partner will help you let go of the relationship in peace and without as much remorse or regret.

351. Is divorce the right choice for me?

352. What expectations, blame, fear, or judgement about this relationship do I need to release to end this relationship in peace and with integrity?

353. What is most important for me to learn about myself as this relationship ends?

354. As divorce concludes, how do I proceed in my life? What is my next step?

355. What is my path to greater happiness within relationship?

---

## RECONCILIATION IN RELATIONSHIP

Especially after a period of struggle, separation, or parting, there may be an opportunity to reconcile. In this moment, often the best course is to return to the relationship with open eyes, checking what denial you may have harbored, what pain, blame, or anger you may hold. Address issues first before agreeing to the reconciliation, thereby creating a path which serves both going forward.

356. Are my partner and I both in integrity with reconciling?

357. Am I giving up myself to reconcile? How?

358. What agreements or understandings do we need to encourage success in re-establishing a relationship?

359. How can we shift our communication to support our relationship moving forward?

360. What is my responsibility for the success of this new chapter in our relationship?

361. What three things can I do for myself as we move forward?

362. What three things can I do for my partner as we move forward?

363. What am I not seeing about reconciling?

364. What can I understand about myself within the prospects of this effort at reconciliation?

---

## FAMILY

Love them, hate them – can't live with them, can't live without them. Family is where you grow up, family is created in marriage, and family can be the group you create for yourself beyond biological lines. Within the dynamics of the family everyone has a different experience, everyone has different intentions, everyone has different triggers for anger, excitement, or growth.

365. Within the dynamics of our family, what supports each of us?

366. How do the dynamics of my family trigger me?

367. What will improve the vitality of our family relationship?

368. What dynamic within my family is the source of my anger or pain?

369. What can I do to help move my family into a healthy, positive relationship for all?

370. What do I need to understand about my role in my family?

371.What do I need to shift around my beliefs about family?

CHILDREN

As a parent, the desire and the challenge is to love and support the child so that the child feels loved and wanted and is capable of growing into a loving, responsible, and honest adult. Each child needs something different, and what is needed is not the same from both parents. The path is not always clear and needs shift over time.

372. What is the root issue of my frustration with my kids?

373. What can I do to shift the relationship with my kids so that we experience joy?

374. What can I do for my child to deepen the connection we share?

375. What activities can I bring to my children which will expand their growth and improve our relationships?

376. What is the relationship with my child about for me at the soul level?

377. What is the one thing I can do for my child which is most beneficial for my child?

378. What does my child need from me to grow into a loving, responsible, honest and happy adult?

379. As my child moves from childhood to young adulthood, what is the most beneficial support that I can offer?

380. How am I holding my child back?

381. What makes me feel like my kids don't listen to me?

382. How can I shift what I say so that my kids listen to me?

383. What can I do to shift the relationship with my kids so that conflict is reduced and happiness for us all increased?

---

## IN-LAWS

The relationship dynamics with in-laws can be deep and loving, complicated and challenging. Depending on the state of your relationship, there will be nuances which influence your relationship in both positive and negative ways.

384. What is the truth of my relationship with my in-laws?

385. What steps can I take to release tension and improve my relationship with my in-laws?

386. What is the source of tension and challenge with my in-laws?

387. How do the dynamics of the relationship with my partner affect the relationship with my in-laws?

388. What do my in-laws want from me within our relationship?

389. How can I include my in-laws in the activities of our family?

390. How can I facilitate a positive relationship between my children and my in-laws?

391. As I move toward separation or divorce, what can I do to maintain a positive relationship with my in-laws?

392. In separation or divorce is maintaining a relationship with my in-laws advisable? Why and how?

# SADNESS

393. What is the source of my sadness?

394. What can help me shift away from feeling sad?

395. Do I hold on to my feelings of sadness to protect myself or ignore another issue?

396. Is my sadness a symptom of a deeper issue or feeling?

---

# SEXUAL CHALLENGES AND OPPORTUNITIES

397. What can I do to increase my enjoyment of my sex life?

398. Why do I feel resistant to engaging in sex with my partner?

399. How can I connect on a deeper, more intimate level with my partner?

400. How am I disconnected from the feelings of my body?

401. In what way does my body image interfere with sexual pleasure?

# TIREDNESS OR LACK OF SLEEP

402. Why do I feel tired much of the time?

403. What will restore me so that I don't feel tired?

404. Why do I have trouble sleeping (falling asleep, staying asleep)?

405. What stress am I carrying that is keeping me from feeling refreshed from sleep?

406. Are there other burdens which hinder sleep?

407. Are there physical or emotional challenges which are interfering with my ability to sleep or to feel rested?

408. How does stress wear me out and reduce my resiliency?

409. Is there something about my bedroom or my home which hinders my ability to get a good night's sleep?

# TIRED OF THERAPY

410. What can I understand about myself that will help me feel better about my life?

411. Why do I feel that I have come to a dead-end with therapy or with my therapist?

412. What will help me feel that I can move forward in my life?

413. In therapy, what is holding me back?

# TRAUMA

414. Why do I feel held back by a traumatic event that happened to my childhood?

415. What can I understand and release about this event that would allow me to move on?

416. What pain, fear, anger, or trauma keeps me from awareness of wholeness, balance, and clear connection in my life?

## UNFOCUSED, LACK OF CONCENTRATION:

417. Why am I unfocused and finding concentration difficult?

418. What will improve my focus and concentration?

419. Where do I need to turn my attention?

# UNHAPPY

420. What is the truth of my unhappiness?

421. Why does happiness seem elusive for me?

422. What unrealistic expectations keep me from experiencing happiness in my life?

423. At what moments in my life have I experienced happiness?

424. What is happiness for me?

425. What steps can I take to claim happiness in my life?

# VICTIM OF CRIME

426. What can I learn from this incident in my life?

427. How can I best process my pain, guilt, anger, or shame related to this incident?

428. What can I do to move forward, beyond this incident?

---

# INVITATION

The Akashic Records have become the way I have written the story of my soul in each minute of my day and in every experience of my life. I have learned to trust myself and believe in myself. I am much better at dealing with trouble and the unexpected, so neither rips me apart as they once did.

I often refer to the opening of the Akashic Records as the soul's spiritual practice. Over twenty years of practice, my experience with the Akashic Records has expanded my view of myself, opened my heart and mind, and nourished my body and soul. Always a process of trust and truth that fuels me and supports the best of me always.

I'm not who I was twenty or thirty years ago – but now I'm more me than I have ever been. Not because I swallowed the magic pill of the Akashic Records. Instead, because I picked me for me and have lived MY life. Over and over, I have had to choose me instead of fear, instead of self-judgment, and instead of the illusion of the *right answer*. The Akashic Records did not make me perfect. But my connection with this sacred flow pointed me in the direction of my truth and the choices I can make knowing me.

I hope that the Questions Suggestions in this book help you touch your heart and understand your soul. Remember there are no *perfect* or *right* questions — just the question you know is for you to ask in the moment. Trust yourself!

If you'd like to learn more about the Akashic Records, here are two possibilities:

---

*10+ Secrets of the Akashic Records* - transforms the Akashic Records from a simplistic advice book to a personal process of learning and growth.

*Akashic Records Master Course* - the best step-by-step guide to learn how to open the Akashic Records for yourself and for others.

---

Or join my newsletter.

Your truth may not be found in the path of the Akashic Records. In whatever way calls to you, may you find your truth and a life of laughter, learning, and love.

In Joy!

Cheryl

# ABOUT CHERYL

**www.cherylmarlene.com**

Cheryl Marlene is all about soul perspective, heart connection, and deep knowing.

The world's authority on the Akashic Records, she is also a mystic who is unafraid of the tough, the raw, and the real aspects of doing deep work. She conducts Readings and teaches students to access the Akashic Records through her signature *Akashic Records Master Course*. In the field of consciousness, she is known as a futurist, innovator, and master teacher who delivers life-changing lessons with warmth and humor. Her exploration takes her to the cutting edge: bringing the future to you today, to help prepare you for what you will need tomorrow.

Cheryl's clients and students know her as a relatable, funny, everyday person who loves red dresses, urban fantasy books, and skinny margaritas. She is also an avid hiker. Her claim for herself is poetic soul, sharp mind, beautiful body, open heart.

Laugh. Learn. Love. Be. Become. Always.

**Cheryl's Books:**

10+ Secrets of the Akashic Records

400+ Questions to Ask the Akashic Records

Affirmations Power Personal Transformation

How to Navigate the Five Steps of Your Spiritual Journey

CHERYL MARLENE

**Akashic Records Master Course**

Introduction to the Akashic Records

Open Your Akashic Records

Open the Akashic Records for Other

Soul Energy Dynamics and the Akashic Records

Healing and the Akashic Records

Manufactured by Amazon.ca
Bolton, ON

18643172R00050